SRA Early Interventions in Reading

The Jumbled Journey

By
Becky Allen

Illustrated by
Robert Casilla

Columbus, OH

The **McGraw·Hill** Companies

Photo Credits

35 ©Kike Calvo/Bruce Coleman, Inc.

MHEonline.com

 SRA

Imprint 2012

Copyright © 2005 by SRA/McGraw-Hill.

Send all inquiries to:
SRA/McGraw-Hill
8787 Orion Place
Columbus, OH 43240-4027

Printed in the United States

ISBN 0-07-604474-2

7 8 9 DOC 15 14 13

Contents

Chapter 1
Our Journey Begins

For months our family had been planning an unforgettable trip to England with the Hamiltons. My name is Polly, and I have a younger brother named Josh. My best friend is Theresa Hamilton, and she has two older brothers named Tobias and Cameron. My parents and Mr. and Mrs. Hamilton and all the kids were going to England together!

At last the day to leave New York arrived. I was ecstatic with happiness. It was exciting walking through the airport on the way to our gate.

As we walked onto the plane, the flight attendant made an announcement: "Welcome aboard our 777!"

We couldn't believe our eyes. Our plane was huge!

"Let's find our seats," Mrs. Hamilton urged. "We're in the twenty-third row."

With four adults and five children, we filled a row of nine comfortable seats. Soon the engines roared, and the plane tore down the runway.
In six hours we would be in London. I wondered what I would do for six hours.

"Look!" Theresa said. She pointed to a screen hanging from the ceiling. "We can watch movies to pass the time."

"Not until you've had your lunch," the flight attendant said, placing trays with soup and a sandwich in front of me, Theresa, and everyone else.

"Yum!" said Tobias. "This is going to be an incredible trip!"

The hours went fast. Soon the plane landed in London, and we took a taxi to our hotel. I felt a great sense of awareness. I couldn't believe we were in England!

The following morning we were eager to explore. I couldn't wait to go to our first stop—the impeccable Buckingham Palace, where the queen of England lives. A real queen!

"The fastest way to reach the palace is on the subway. The British call the subway the tube," Dad explained.

I didn't know what to expect as Dad led us to a street corner and then down a staircase.

We were in an underground tunnel full of emptiness. Mom pointed to a map on the wall of possible train routes.

"Do you see how each subway route is a different color?" she asked. "We need to get on the green line."

Quickly a sleek, modern train pulled up, and we climbed aboard. Whoosh! The train immediately shot into the tunnel.

Soon we arrived at St. James's Park, which is just across from Buckingham Palace. On the way to the palace, something peculiar happened. Josh stumbled over a loose brick in the pathway. When he knelt to fix the brick, he found a flat, inexpensive tin box beneath it. Inside the box were a beautiful pin that looked like a butterfly and a handwritten note. Josh read it.

"'Please see that my daughter gets this gold pin,'" Josh read. "'Her name is Nora Banks, and she lives in Naples, Italy. I'm unable to send this to her. Thank you for your help.'" Josh looked up. "It's signed 'Joseph Banks.'"

What were we to do? It sounded like a fascinating adventure to me, even though it would mean a little craziness.

My parents and Mr. and Mrs. Hamilton talked for a short while. My mom had tenderness in her eyes, and I could tell she was considering taking the pin to Nora. After a few minutes, the adults looked at the children, and the children looked at the adults, and we all instantly knew—we were going to Italy to help Joseph Banks!

Chapter 2
Train Tracks to Naples

We decided to leave for Naples the next day and return to London later. To get to Naples, we first took a train to Paris, France.

"This train uses the 'Chunnel' to reach France," Mrs. Hamilton explained. "The Chunnel is an underwater tunnel. It passes under the English Channel."

I clapped my hands with happiness. We were going on an underwater train!

We filed into the train and found our seats. A young woman with a cart offered us snacks.

I began to get impatient, but before long the train entered the Chunnel, and the area outside the window turned black. We pressed our faces against the glass but saw nothing. I thought about all the water that must be floating around the tunnel walls and felt a little nervousness. Fifteen minutes later we reappeared in the daylight.

"We're in France!" Josh cheered. But we still had a terribly long way to go. The train started to go faster and faster. My dad said it was going 186 miles per hour!

When the three-hour trip ended, we bought tickets for our next ride. The trip from Paris to Naples would take more than fourteen hours in a regular train.

We stayed in private cabins on a night train and slept soundly in our bunks. The next day we were in Naples. I was so excited. The weather was beautiful, and the trees were very green.

We located Nora's address; she lived high above the city. A man on the street told us that Nora's home was inaccessible—except by funicular. What is a funicular?

The man pointed to the next corner, and we walked over and looked up.

"Look! The cars move along a cable," Tobias said. We watched the funicular climb the visibly steep hill. "Too bad it's inside a tunnel. We'd have such a great view."

We got on the funicular. I was glad we didn't have to climb steps instead!

Nora Banks owned an inn at the top of the hill. We introduced ourselves and explained that we had come a long way to find her.

When Nora saw the pin, she burst into tears. "My goodness, this is impossible. This was my mother's," she said. "Who gave this to you?"

Mrs. Hamilton told her about the box Josh had found and the note.

"My father had to give all his belongings to a nursing home," Nora said. "He had no other way to pay for his care."

"Your father must have loved you very much," my mother said gently. "The pin must have been special to him too."

Nora wiped away her tears and smiled. "I can't tell you how much this means to me. You've come such a long way. Won't you please stay for dinner?"

We did stay, and we ate homemade Italian spaghetti. It was indescribably delicious!

The next day we planned our return trip to England so we could continue our trip, but first we went to see some sights around Naples. We explored a castle, toured a museum, and shopped for souvenirs. In the middle of the afternoon, Cameron saw an elderly man sitting alone on a park bench.

"Are you okay?" he asked, approaching him. "I don't mean to be impolite, but you seem lost and full of sadness."

"I'm trying to get to Egypt," the man said. "My granddaughter needs my help."

We learned that the man—his name was Ahmed—had already traveled many miles. He was horribly tired and hungry, so the Hamiltons got him something to eat and offered him a bed in their hotel room.

That night we all agreed—we would travel to Egypt to take Ahmed to his granddaughter.

Chapter 3
Another Change of Plans

The next morning we went to the docks in Naples and climbed onto a ferry that would carry us across the sea to northern Africa. The ferry was a large white ship with three levels. It transported people as well as automobiles, small trucks, and bicycles. We sat on the top level where we could eat, relax, and enjoy the transportation.

When the ferry reached land, its horn bellowed with boldness. Then Mr. Hamilton gave an explanation about the next leg of the trip. "Now we have to cross miles of desert," he said. "And I thought a fun way to make the trip would be on the backs of camels!"

Our mouths fell open in disbelief.

"Wow!" Josh yelled, grinning. "I'm more than ready for that!"

It wasn't long before we found a guide with camels. The guide gave us each a cloth to wind around our heads and faces for protection against the hot sun and sand.

Then the camels knelt down for us to mount. As the camels plodded along, they swayed back and forth incessantly. "This is like riding on a boat," said Tobias, gripping the saddle.

My eyes began to hurt from looking at the sun's reflection on the bright sand. I looked at the camel's eyes—he had two sets of eyelashes! Pretty spectacular.

My mom threw a bottle of suntan lotion to me, and I put some on my arms and face. Miles and miles of sand stretched out before me. It was emptiness, but it was gorgeous!

At night we built a couple of fires and used them to cook our food, and then we slept in tents. The camels had carried our suitcases and supplies.

After many days of motion we finally arrived in the village where Ahmed's granddaughter lived. Ahmed ran to greet the impressive young girl. "These people have helped me find you," Ahmed said. "Now we can be together."

Before long, we bid farewell to Ahmed and his granddaughter. Then, instead of taking the camels back, we took a bus to the nearest airport.

We hoped we might return to England, but when we reached the ticket counter, something was wrong that needed our attention. Mom's suitcase was missing. She had picked up an incorrect bag—a bag that had a tag with an address of a person from China!

"This bag belongs to someone named Ping Chen," Mom said. "And I bet he has my bag."

"Quick!" Mr. Hamilton urged. "The next flight for Hong Kong leaves in ten minutes. To get your bag back, we need to return Mr. Ping's."

We dashed to the plane. In no time, we were jetting off across Asia. I laughed with happiness. This was some vacation!

When we arrived in Hong Kong, it was immediately humming with life. The air was full of conversation and vibration. Everyone seemed to be going somewhere.

We climbed onto a bus and then, later in the day, rented rickshaws, which are two-wheeled wagons that carry people. But instead of horses pulling the rickshaws, people on bikes pull them!

"I feel like a kid again," Mr. Hamilton announced with jubilation as he rode past us. "This is like riding on a big tricycle."

We sat in the covered cabs, enjoying the ride and the city buzzing around us. We passed many businesses and restaurants.

"What a great way to travel!" Theresa shouted gleefully. "Lots of fresh air."

In the tiny town of Li Pei, we found Ping Chen working in his yard. He and Mom were glad to get their bags back. Mom had missed her favorite shoes, and Mr. Ping had needed his robe.

That night we stayed with Mr. Ping. There was a celebration going on in town, and at first we were indecisive, but Mr. Ping convinced us to join the party.

There was a long dragon winding its way through the action in the streets. The costume was full of vivid colors, and the people underneath carrying the dragon were full of craziness! The dragon slithered along as if it were really alive.

We had a wonderful time, but the next day we were off on a train to the airport. We would try again to return to England.

Chapter 4
A Rain Forest Find

"This looks like something out of the future," Josh remarked as we climbed onto the maglev train. The modern white train sped to the airport at an incredible 265 miles per hour! But there were no wheels or engines. Powerful magnets lifted the train above the track and silently thrust it forward.

I giggled with Theresa. "Wow! This is like flying!" I said. She agreed with my opinion.

At the airport we stopped at a snack bar. The flight to England would be long, and we were famished. At the table next to us, a young woman seemed like she was in distress and suffering from dizziness. She coughed and wheezed, trying to catch her breath.

Mrs. Hamilton leaned over and gently asked, "Are you okay? Is there something we can do to help?"

"I'm sorry to bother you," the woman replied. "I have an unusual illness. The only cure is to drink a special kind of tea made from the leaves of a rare plant from the Australian rain forest. But I'm too weak to go find the plant. It's impossible for me to go that far."

Mrs. Hamilton sighed and turned to us. We all knew what she was about to say.

There was no doubt about it—
we were off on another vacation
detour. We took a flight to an airport
near the Australian rain forest and
then rented two cars and drove north.

"I can't get used to riding on the
left side of the road," Mom said.

"You should try steering from the
right side of the car," Dad replied.

It really was strange to drive this way, but the views were too much of a distraction for me to notice. The highway to the rain forest stretched along the coast. The ocean was turquoise blue. Within a day we arrived at the edge of the rain forest. It was breathtaking, with millions of huge, glistening plants and the smell of wet soil.

To find the rare plant, we had to enter the heart of the forest. A guide suggested taking the Skyrail, which would carry us just above the treetops and then deep into the most inaccessible parts of the jungle.

Each family climbed into a small cabin that hung from a thick cable, and then we glided up the impressive mountain.

We caught an outstanding view of the valley and the sea below. As we swayed above the treetops, I slid open the cabin window. "Listen to all the amazing sounds," I said. "This place is really alive!"

Soon the Skyrail carried us to the forest floor, and we climbed out.

"Now search for a small red flower with five petals," Mom explained with determination.

Chapter 5
Along the Amazon

We crawled under shrubs and pushed back clumps of ferns. Soon Tobias squealed with delight. "I found some!" he yelled like a champion. We picked just the leaves of the plants and placed them into a mailing pouch.

On our way back to the Skyrail, I made a decision and stopped. I stood on the floor of the rain forest, looking around and thinking quietly to myself.

To think—just a few days ago I had been in New York, and now I'd been all over the world! I thought about all the cultures and lives that were so different from mine. They had made such an impression on me. All this because of a simple trip to England!

On the way back to the airport, we mailed the leaves to the woman in China, with the hope that they would help with her illness.

Before returning our rental car, Dad stopped at a gas station and filled the car with gas. A man at the station approached us with a panicked expression on his face.

"Please help me," the man begged. "My granddaughter in Brazil was injured in a fall and cannot walk. A doctor in New York can help her, but Taki has no way of getting there."

We had been traveling like crazy for days, but our incessant adventures had not ended. We were tireless! Our next stop was along the Amazon River in Brazil—the home of this nice man's granddaughter.

Once we reached Brazil, we had to cruise up the river to reach Taki's village. After a bit of discussion, two natives offered us a ride in their canoes carved from solid logs.

As the men paddled, we skimmed over the muddy waters, but it was hard work. We were moving against the current.

I looked for something to block the harsh sunlight, but the boat offered little comfort—not even seats. Instead, we sat cross-legged on the hard floor as the sounds of gurgling water trickled past us on our important mission.

Our voyage ended near a grove of rubber trees. I learned that the sap of rubber trees is used to make rubber.

"We'll need to ride mules for the rest of our excursion," Mom explained.

Our mules had no saddles or stirrups. Dad helped Theresa and me onto the animal's back. Mom rode behind us and held the reins as the mule walked to our next destination.

The mules carried us into the hills. It was a slow but steady journey. Cameron patted his mule's neck as it plodded along. "Sorry to load you down like this," he whispered.

I thought of the camels in Egypt and tried to make a decision. Did I like camels or mules better?

Within a few hours, we arrived at Taki's village. Her grandfather was filled with happiness.

Taki was waiting with an expression of disbelief. Her grandfather hugged her and lifted her onto a mule, and we all returned to the river, this time catching a large ship that carried us all the way to the sea, where we headed north toward New York— home! Taki and her grandfather made it to her doctor, but we never did make it back to England.

Am I sorry? Absolutely not! Our jumbled journey was wonderful! I've never had so much excitement on a vacation.